W9-DDC-222

Exploring ENERGY

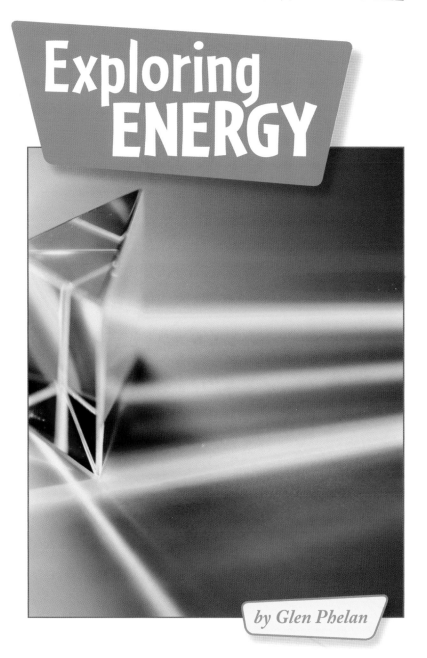

by Glen Phelan

sundance™

Program written and developed by Kate Boehm Jerome
in association with Sundance Publishing.

Editorial, Design, and Production by Baseline Development Group
in association with Sundance Publishing.

Consultant/Reviewer: Rebecca L. Johnson, Science Writer, Sioux Falls, SD

Published by
Sundance Publishing
33 Boston Post Road West
Suite 440
Marlborough, MA 01752
800-343-8204
www.sundancepub.com

Photography:
Cover © Paul A. Souders/CORBIS; p. 1 Lawrence Lawry/Photo Researchers, Inc.; p. 3 © Paul A. Souders/CORBIS; pp. 4-5 © Bill Stormont/CORBIS; p. 6 © Joe McBride/CORBIS; p. 7 (left) © Royalty-Free/CORBIS, (right) Johner/Getty Images; p. 8 (left) Photodisc/Getty Images, (right) PhotoSpin, Inc/Alamy; p. 9 (top) Cheryl Clegg/Index Stock Imagery, (bottom) Danita Delimont/Alamy; p. 10 (top) Tetra Images/Alamy, (center) © Alan Schein/zefa/CORBIS, (bottom) Fred Hirschmann/Getty Images; p. 11 (top) © Michelle Pedone/zefa/CORBIS, (center left) © Paul Freytag/zefa/CORBIS, (center right) © Royalty-Free/CORBIS, (bottom) Photodisc/Getty Images; p. 12 (left) JGI/Getty Images, (right) www.dominodomain.com; p. 13 White Cross Productions/Getty Images; p. 14 © Tom Stewart/CORBIS; p. 15 (both) © 1985 Richard Megna/Fundamental Photographs, NYC; p. 16 Michael Dzaman/Alamy; p. 17 (top) © T. Hemmings/zefa/CORBIS, (bottom) Bryan Mullennix/Getty Images; p. 18 © Al Francekevich/CORBIS; p. 19 © Royalty-Free/CORBIS; p. 20 Lawrence Lawry/Photo Researchers, Inc.; p. 21 © Bill Ross/CORBIS; p. 22 Bernhard Edmaier/Photo Researchers, Inc.; p. 24 (top) AP/Wide World Photos, (bottom) © Roger Ressmeyer/CORBIS; p. 25 © George Steinmetz/CORBIS; p. 26 © Dietrich Rose/zefa/CORBIS; p. 27 © Walter Geiersperger/ CORBIS; p. 29 (top) © Royalty-Free/CORBIS

Illustration:
p. 23 Hanh Luu

ISBN: 978-1-4207-0349-8

Printed in China
08/09-225494

Cover photo: A static electricity display at Ontario Science Center

Table of Contents

Down on the Farm

Imagine spending a few days on a farm. You stroll through a field of golden wheat. The sun feels warm on your shoulders. The wind blows the tall shafts of wheat.

Suddenly the calm is broken by a roar that grows louder. You turn around. A combine is rolling your way. This huge machine has long, swirling blades that cut the wheat and a powerful engine that runs on diesel fuel.

But diesel fuel is not the only source of energy on this farm. Believe it or not, everything you see, hear, and feel involves energy. This includes the sun, the wind, and even the wheat. And that's just the beginning.

CHAPTER 1

Energy Basics

A swimmer pushes off the side of the pool with a burst of energy. He'll need plenty of it to win the race. You need energy for the things that you do, too. And you don't even have to be swimming in a race. In fact, you need energy to sit and read this book. What is this thing called energy?

Energy All Around

Energy is the ability to do work. That's a simple sentence. But what does it mean? Think about turning on a light. You raise your hand to the light switch. To do this, you change the position of your hand. This action requires energy. And this energy comes from your body.

Next, you flip the switch, changing its position. This motion of flipping the switch uses energy. Then, as the electricity flows through the wire, more changes are caused by energy.

Finally, the electricity changes the light bulb. The **electrical energy** makes the filament inside the bulb get hot and begin to glow.

Those are a lot of changes just to turn on a light. And each change requires energy. Does every action and every change always involve energy? The answer is yes!

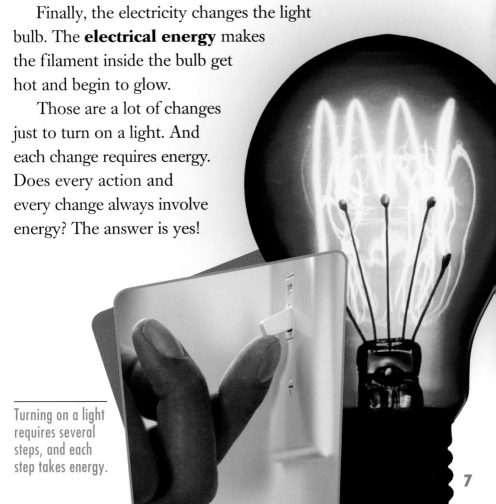

Turning on a light requires several steps, and each step takes energy.

7

Kinetic Energy

Sometimes it's easy to tell that an object has energy. If it's moving, it has energy. This energy of motion is called **kinetic energy.**

Think about it! A speeding train, a fiery rocket, and a rushing waterfall all have kinetic energy. So does a fluttering leaf and a crawling baby. Even your eyes have kinetic energy as they move back and forth to read the words on this page.

A fast-moving object has more kinetic energy than a slow-moving object. Also, a heavy object has more kinetic energy than a light object. Which object shown here has more kinetic energy?

A rocket is much heavier and faster moving, so it has more kinetic energy than a dog.

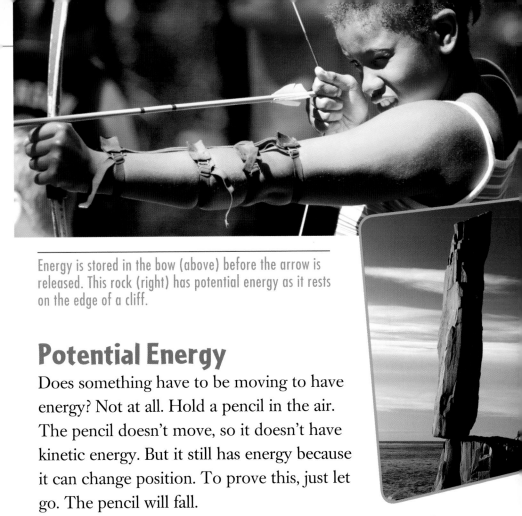

Energy is stored in the bow (above) before the arrow is released. This rock (right) has potential energy as it rests on the edge of a cliff.

Potential Energy

Does something have to be moving to have energy? Not at all. Hold a pencil in the air. The pencil doesn't move, so it doesn't have kinetic energy. But it still has energy because it can change position. To prove this, just let go. The pencil will fall.

When you hold the pencil in the air, it has **potential energy,** or energy that is stored. Anything that can fall, or be pulled down by gravity, has potential energy.

An object that is squeezed or stretched also has potential energy. Did you ever "shoot" a rubber band by hooking it on your thumb and stretching it? The farther you stretch it, the more potential energy you give it. When you release the rubber band, you release its potential, or stored, energy.

Some objects have potential energy because of the chemicals that make them up. That's how energy is stored in food. When food molecules break apart in your body, they release the stored energy that your body uses.

9

Different Forms of Energy

Mechanical energy is energy that moves objects. You use mechanical energy when you hit a baseball.

Electrical energy, or electricity, is the movement of tiny, charged particles called electrons. Electrical energy powers many of the machines you use every day, including lights, TVs, and computers.

Electromagnetic energy travels in waves. This kind of energy includes visible light–the light that we can see. Other kinds of **electromagnetic energy** include X-rays, microwaves, infrared radiation, and ultraviolet light. Most of this energy comes from the sun.

Sound energy comes from the vibration of particles in a solid, a liquid, or a gas. You hear most sounds because your ears detect vibrations in the air made by **sound energy.**

Chemical energy is energy that is stored in the chemicals that make up a substance. The energy is released when that substance is broken down or undergoes a chemical change—such as when fireworks are burned.

Thermal energy comes from the moving particles that make up matter. The atoms and molecules that make up you, this book, the air, and all matter are constantly moving. The faster they move, the warmer the matter feels.

Nuclear energy is stored inside an atom. When the center, or nucleus, breaks apart, or when nuclei join together, energy is released. The sun's energy comes from the joining of nuclei, or nuclear fusion.

Energy on the Move

The sound of dominoes knocking each other down is the sound of energy on the move. You give the first domino a little push. That energy makes it tip over. It hits the next domino and passes its energy along. In this way, the energy from your push travels through the whole line of dominoes.

Energy not only moves from place to place, it also converts, or changes, to other forms. In fact, most actions involve **energy conversions.**

Think about the dominoes again. Your body converts the **chemical energy** in food into **mechanical energy** to move your muscles. You gave some of this mechanical energy to the first domino. Most of this energy was passed along the line of dominoes. But some of it was converted to sound. And with each hit, a tiny bit of the mechanical energy also turned into **thermal energy**–or **heat.**

The mechanical energy of the push of the person's finger converts to mechanical, sound, and thermal energy.

Building with dominoes takes concentration and leaves no room for error.

Think about all the changes that happen when you clap your hands. Those changes involve energy conversions.

Chemical energy of food → Mechanical energy of clapping → Sound energy and thermal energy from hands hitting together

So how does food get its chemical energy? Good question! Plants use the sun's energy to grow. If we eat a plant, the energy the plant contains is transferred to us. If a cow eats a plant, and then we eat a hamburger, the energy has been transferred from the plant to the cow to us.

BLUE PLANET Note

No matter how often energy changes form, the total amount of energy stays the same. So the chemical energy in a match is equal to the light, heat, and sound given off when the match burns.

CHAPTER 2

Focus on Heat and Light

When the sun sets, with it goes the bright light and the heat of day. The camp turns dark and cold. Luckily a roaring fire soon blazes. The light and heat energy from the fire make the campsite more enjoyable again.

Matter on the Move

Remember, the tiny particles that make up all matter are constantly moving. Therefore everything has some amount of thermal energy. The more thermal energy an object has, the faster the particles move and the warmer it is.

Which flask of liquid has more thermal energy? On the left, the liquid is still, so the particles are moving more slowly. On the right, the liquid is bubbling, and the particles are moving rapidly.

You see thermal energy in action all the time! In fact, a simple demonstration can show you that warmer water has more thermal energy than cooler water. Put a drop of food coloring into a cup of warm water. Then put a drop of food coloring into a cup of cool water. What will happen to the food coloring?

The particles in the warm water move faster than the particles in the cool water. This means the drop of food coloring will spread out faster in the warm water than in the cool water.

The Heat Is On

In comparing the cups of cool and warm water, it is clear that the warm water has more thermal energy. But if you asked which cup has more heat, the answer is neither. Heat is not something an object *has*. It is something an object *gives off*. Heat is the flow of thermal energy from warmer matter to cooler matter. Heat is one way energy moves from one place to another.

For example, when wood burns, its stored chemical energy changes to thermal energy. The thermal energy flows away from the fire as heat. A wood stove produces heat as the thermal energy moves through the air and to your skin.

The thermal energy of the fire moves away from the fire as heat. This heat cooks the food on the grill.

Have you ever started to eat a spoonful of warm soup, only to find that it's already cold? You know that hot food cools off, but how does it happen?

It all has to do with particles and heat! The particles that make up the hot soup are moving fast. They are mostly vibrating, or jiggling back and forth, at lightning speed. The particles in the cooler air and the cooler bowl are moving more slowly. The food particles collide with the particles in the bowl and in the air. The collisions transfer some of the food's thermal energy. The food particles slow down while the bowl and air particles speed up. So the food gets cooler while the bowl and the air just above the food get warmer. Heat has flowed from the warmer matter to the cooler matter. After a while, everything will be at room temperature.

Blowing on a hot drink moves the air directly above the hot liquid and speeds up heat transfer.

BLUE PLANET Note

How does a Styrofoam™ cup keep your hot cocoa warm on a cool day? The Styrofoam slows down the process of heat loss. But eventually, the liquid in the cup will reach the same temperature as the air around it.

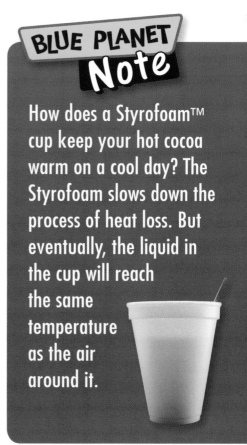

Sources of Heat

Have you ever rubbed your hands together on a cold day? The friction, or rubbing, produces heat that warms your hands. Any objects that move against one another produce heat. That's why engines get so hot. Many of the parts rub against one another very quickly.

Most forms of energy produce heat. When you rub your hands together, you are converting mechanical energy to heat. Electrical energy converts to heat in lightbulbs, electric stoves, irons, and other appliances. Chemical energy converts to heat when something burns. The most important source of heat for Earth is the sun. And it is also our most important source of light.

Friction between a match and a rough surface produces enough heat to ignite the chemicals on the head of the match.

Light travels in waves away from its source in all directions.

Turn On the Light

Imagine being in a basement at night. It's totally dark. You pull a cord, and an overhead lightbulb goes on. Suddenly the entire basement lights up.

How can one little bulb light up a whole room? Simple. Light doesn't stay put. It travels outward in waves. It moves away from the source in all directions. The light waves bounce off objects and reach our eyes. Our brain receives the light waves as signals. Then we can see things. All this happens so quickly that we don't even realize it.

As you know, most light on Earth comes from the sun. Unlike sound waves, light waves can travel through empty space. That's good because sunlight doesn't just light up our world. It also gives plants what they need to make their own food.

Light bends, or refracts, inside a prism, separating into the colors that you see in a rainbow.

The Color of Light

Have you ever noticed a patch of colors on the floor as sunlight shines through a window? Maybe you've seen colors in soap bubbles, on top of an oily puddle, or in the spray of a garden hose. In each instance, the pattern of colors is the same as in a rainbow. What's going on?

The sunlight that we see is visible light. This light looks white, or colorless. However, it is really a combination of many different colors. Each color has a different **wavelength,** which is the distance between two identical, repeating peaks in a wave.

When white light travels through a clear material such as a glass of water, the light bends, or **refracts.** Different wavelengths of light refract by different amounts. This action separates the light into its different colors. The separated colors that we can see are red, orange, yellow, green, blue, indigo, and violet. The order of these colors is always the same, whether in a rainbow or a soap bubble.

How come different objects are different colors? Different objects reflect and absorb different wavelengths of light. For example, a leaf looks green because it reflects, or bounces back, green wavelengths to your eyes. The leaf absorbs, or takes in, the other wavelengths of light.

White objects reflect all wavelengths of light. Black objects absorb all wavelengths of light. Look around you. What colors are being absorbed and reflected?

We see the rose as yellow because wavelengths of yellow light reflect to our eyes.

CHAPTER 3

Putting Energy to Use

Rising 726 feet (221 meters) above the Colorado River, the Hoover Dam is one of the largest dams in the world. The dam provides water for irrigation and controls flooding downstream. But its most important purpose is to provide electricity to much of California, Nevada, and Arizona.

Generating Electricity

Some of the most important uses of energy are to operate our lights, computers, and other electrical equipment. Most of the electricity we use is produced in **electrical generators.** In these machines, strong magnets spin around loops of wire. This action produces electricity. The trick is how to make the magnets spin. One way is by using the energy of falling water. That's where a dam becomes useful.

When a dam is built on a river, it seals off the flow of water. But structures built into the dam allow the controlled release of water. On some dams, as the water flows down through these structures, it turns the blades of turbines. These turbines are connected to the magnets of a generator. This produces electricity that can either be stored or sent over power lines to be used in surrounding communities.

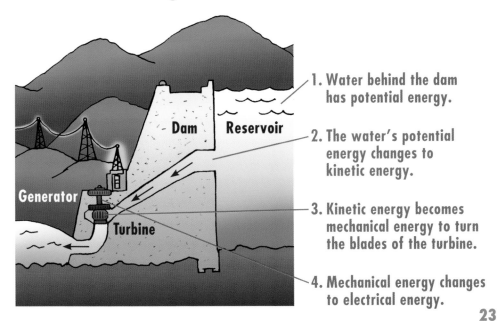

1. Water behind the dam has potential energy.

2. The water's potential energy changes to kinetic energy.

3. Kinetic energy becomes mechanical energy to turn the blades of the turbine.

4. Mechanical energy changes to electrical energy.

23

Fueling Power Plants

Most of the electricity used in the United States doesn't come from water power. Instead it is generated at power plants that burn **fossil fuels.** These are fuels made from plants and animals that lived and died long ago. These fuels include coal, oil, and natural gas.

Power plants that use fossil fuels burn the fuels to heat water. The chemical energy of the fuels changes into thermal energy to boil the water. The kinetic energy of steam from the boiling water turns the turbine and generates electricity.

Coal is a fossil fuel that is used in electrical power plants to generate electricity. It is mined throughout the United States.

So what's all the fuss about fossil fuels? Fossil fuels produce a lot of electricity cheaply, but there are problems. The burning of these fuels adds pollution to the air. Some of the pollution may be changing our climate in dangerous ways. Also, fossil fuels are **nonrenewable** sources of energy. Once they are used up, there are no more.

Another nonrenewable source of energy is **nuclear energy.** In a nuclear power plant, the atoms of a certain kind of metal, called uranium, break apart. This process releases energy, which then heats water to make steam.

Nuclear energy generates about twenty percent of the electricity used in the United States. Some countries, such as France, use nuclear energy even more. A big problem with this energy source is that it produces radioactive wastes that are very dangerous to living things and the environment.

Water vapor is released from a cooling tower at a nuclear power plant.

What Choices Do We Have?

Luckily there are alternatives to nonrenewable energy sources. In fact, you've already read about one of them– the power of falling water. Two others are solar energy and wind energy. These are **renewable** energy sources because they can't be used up.

Solar cells are thin wafers of material that produce electricity when sunlight strikes them. Thousands of solar cells connected together can be placed on a roof to provide electricity for a house.

Solar energy can also be used to generate electricity at power plants. As with fossil fuels, it's all about boiling water. At one kind of solar power plant, mirrors focus sunlight on pipes or tanks that contain water. The water is heated to make steam that will turn the turbine of a generator.

Homes can be fitted with solar cells to help reduce energy costs.

Solar panels

These wind turbines in the Austrian Alps are located in an area with fairly constant winds, making them a good source of renewable energy.

BLUE PLANET Note

The world's largest wind turbine blades are about 202 feet (61.5 meters) long. That's as long as two basketball courts placed end to end.

People have used wind energy for thousands of years, especially for sailing ships and powering windmills. Windmills were once an important part of producing food. As wind turned the blades, rods and gears inside the windmill moved a huge stone that ground grain into flour. Some farms and ranches still use small windmills to move a pipe up and down to pump water out of the ground.

Modern windmills, called **wind turbines,** produce electricity. The twirling blades spin a turbine. Many wind turbines together can produce enough electricity for an entire community.

Currently, it is more expensive to use renewable energy sources than to use nonrenewable sources. Renewable sources have other problems, too. For instance, dams can prevent fish from migrating, thus reducing their populations. Scientists and engineers are working on these problems.

Blue Planet E-Diary Blog

Tuesday: Writing Assignment

Making the Most of Our Energy

Most of us use a lot of energy at home to run machines and provide heat. But a lot of this energy is wasted. When we waste energy, we

- use up fuels faster than necessary
- create more pollution than necessary
- lose money by paying for energy we don't use

Can you be an energy saver instead of an energy waster? Think about all the ways energy is used in your home. Then write a letter to your family members describing how you want to use less energy. You'll be amazed at all the little changes that can add up to big savings.

posted by BluePlanetXpert / 3:45 PM / Comments 0

Instant Message

Subject:
Energy at Home

>**Waste-not:** What is the number one way that energy is wasted in homes?

BluePlanetXpert: Most household energy waste comes from poor insulation. In the winter, warm air escapes through gaps around windows and doors.

>**Waste-not:** What can we do about it?

BluePlanetXpert: Seal leaks around doors and windows, and don't leave the door open if the furnace or air-conditioning is running.

Blue Planet Chat Room

Subject:
Tips for Saving Energy

>**Waste-not:** Hey, guys. BPX says a good way to save energy is to seal doors and windows. Any other ideas?

NRgee: How about putting on a sweatshirt instead of turning up the heat?

cheergrl: I turn off lights that I'm not using.

bearman: Yeah. You wouldn't believe all the stuff we keep on when no one's in the room—lights, TV, CD player.

Glossary

chemical energy energy that is stored in the chemicals that make up a substance

electrical energy electricity, which is the flow of electrons

electrical generators machines that produce electricity when magnets spin around loops of wire

electromagnetic energy visible light and other forms of radiation

energy the ability to do work

energy conversions the changing of energy from one form to another

fossil fuels fuels that are made from plants and animals that died long ago; fuels that can be burned to release their chemical energy

heat the flow of thermal energy

kinetic energy energy of motion

mechanical energy energy that moves objects

nonrenewable unable to be replaced after being used up

nuclear energy energy stored in the nucleus of an atom

potential energy energy that is stored

refracts bends, as waves of light bend when they enter water, glass, and the air

renewable able to be replaced after being used

solar cells devices that convert sunlight into electricity

sound energy energy that comes from the vibration of particles in a solid, liquid, or gas

thermal energy the total amount of energy that comes from the movement of particles in matter

wavelength the distance between two identical, repeating peaks in a wave

wind turbines windmills that use a turbine and generator to turn wind energy into electricity

Index